CONSERVATORY CANADA™

# New Millennium Piano Series
# GRADE 3

Repertoire List Pieces and Studies of Conservatory Canada - Grade 3

© 1999 Conservatory Canada
Published and Distributed by Novus Via Music Group Inc.
Edition updated May 2016
All Rights Reserved

ISBN 978-0-88909-216-7

Novus Via Music Group Inc.
189 Douglas Street, Stratford, Ontario, Canada  N5A 5P8
(519) 273-7520  www.NVmusicgroup.com

cover design:
Robin E. Cook, AOCA

# About the Series

The *New Millennium Piano Series* is the official repertoire books for CONSERVATORY CANADA™ examinations. This graded series, in eleven volumes (Pre-Grade 1 to Grade 10), is designed not only to serve the needs of students, teachers and parents for examinations, but it is also a valuable teaching resource and comprehensive anthology for any pianist. The list pieces have been carefully selected and edited, and represent repertoire from the Baroque, Classical, Romantic/Impressionist and 20th century periods. For your convenience, we have included the list pieces AND studies for each grade in one volume. In choosing the studies, we have not only considered their suitability in building technique, but we have also tried to ensure that they could stand as recital repertoire in their own right. In addition, each volume also includes a graded arrangement of *O Canada* (with words in English and French). Volumes for grades 1 to 8 include a glossary containing a short biography of each composer represented in the volume. CONSERVATORY CANADA™ encourages at least one Canadian composition be performed in every examination. Composers working in Canada are well represented in the series. A small asterisk next to their name identifies them.

# Notes on Editing

Most composers in the Baroque and Classical periods included only sparse dynamic, articulation, tempo and other performance indications in their scores. Where we felt it necessary, we have added suggested markings. Whenever possible, ornaments have been realized using the latest scholarship as guidelines. For the works of J.S. Bach, students are urged to consult Bach's own table of ornaments as given in the volumes for grades 7 to 10. The *New Millennium Piano Series* is not an Urtext edition. All editorial markings, along with fingering and pedaling, are intended to be helpful suggestions rather than a final authority. The choice of tempo is a matter of personal taste, technical ability, and appropriateness of style. Most of our suggested metronome markings are expressed within a range of tempi. In the 19th and 20th centuries, composers of piano music included more performance indications in their scores, and as a consequence, fewer editorial markings have been required.

Slurs are used to indicate legato notes and do not necessarily indicate a phrase. In accordance with Conservatory Canada's policy regarding redundant accidentals, we have followed the practice that a barline cancels an accidental. Unnecessary accidentals following the barline have been used only in exceptional circumstances.

Bearing in mind acceptable performance practices, you are free to use your own judgement and imagination in changing any editorial markings, especially in the areas of dynamics, articulation, fingering, and the discretionary use of pedal.

The pieces in the *New Millennium Piano Series* have been chosen as an introduction to enjoyable repertoire that is fun to play, while at the same time, helps to develop your technique and musicianship. We hope you will explore the broad variety of styles and periods represented in this series. We suggest that you also explore as many pieces and studies as possible before deciding which ones you will perform in an examination or musical evaluation.

# Fingering Suggestions

In an effort to acknowledge the exploration of creative fingering possibilities, alternate fingering suggestions are given in parentheses on the score for your consideration. CONSERVATORY CANADA™ encourages investigation of different fingering possibilities in order to reveal those that are best suited to the individual pianist's hands.

---

*The Conservatory Canada Piano Syllabus gives full details regarding examinations. Students, teachers and parents are advised to consult the most recent syllabus online for current requirements, regulations, procedures and deadlines for application.*
www.conservatorycanada.ca

# TABLE OF CONTENTS

*indicates Canadian composer

**List A**

# Menuet in G

from the *Anna Magdalena Bach Notebook*, Anh. 114

Johann Sebastian Bach
(1685–1750)

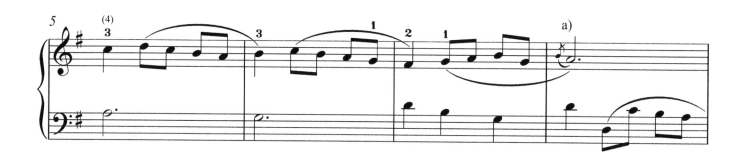

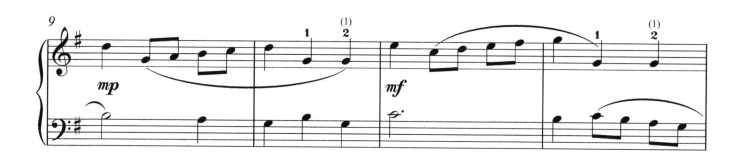

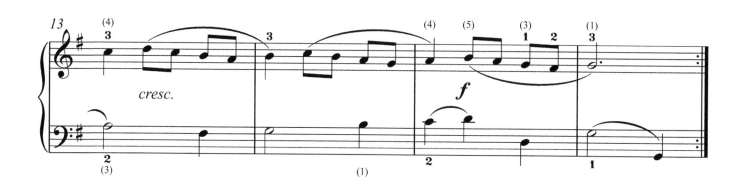

a)  Non-slurred quarter notes may be played detached.

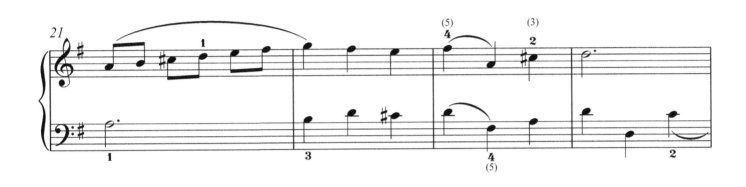

# Menuet in C Minor

from the *Anna Magdalena Bach Notebook*, Anh. 121

Johann Sebastian Bach
(1685–1750)

**List A**

# Musette in D

from the *Anna Magdalena Bach Notebook*, Anh. 126

Johann Sebastian Bach
(1685–1750)

Non-slurred eighth notes may be played detached.

**List A**

# March in C

Jeremiah Clarke
(c1674–1707)

Non-slurred quarter notes may be played detached.

**List A**

# The Fifers

Jean-François Dandrieu
(1682–1738)

Non-slurred eighth notes may be played detached.

# Le Petit Rien
### (The Trifle)

François Couperin
(1668–1733)

Rondeau Légérement
**Allegretto** ♩ = 116–132

Non-slurred quarter notes may be played detached.

# Bourrée in G Minor

Georg Friedrich Händel
(1685–1759)

Non-slurred quarter notes may be played detached.

List A

# Sarabande in B Flat

Johann Pachelbel
(1653–1706)

# Menuet in G

Henry Purcell
(1659–1695)

Non-slurred quarter notes may be played detached.

**List A**

# Gigue

à l'Anglais

Georg Philipp Telemann
(1681–1767)

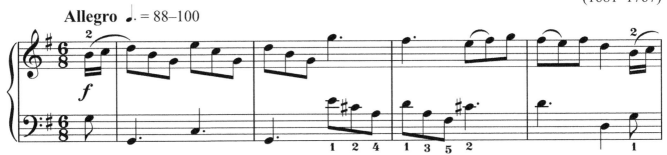

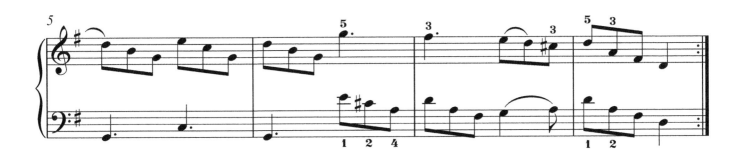

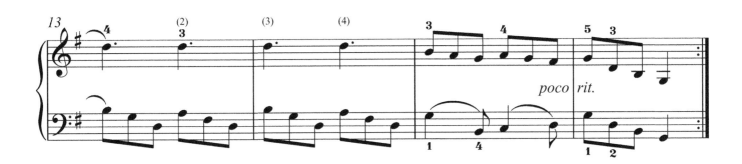

Non-slurred eighth notes may be played detached.

# Gavotte in C

Samuel Arnold
(1740–1802)

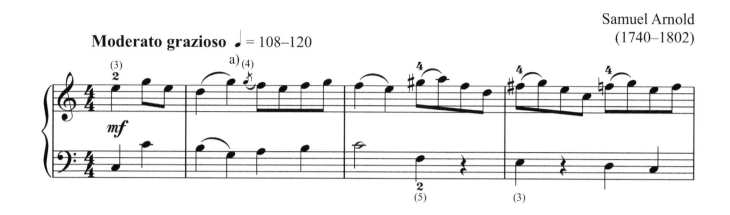

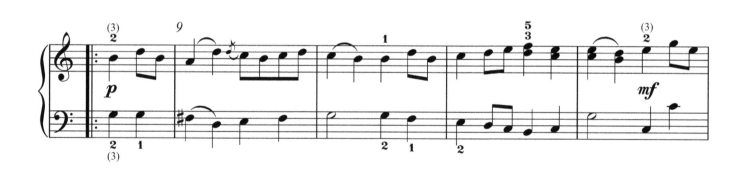

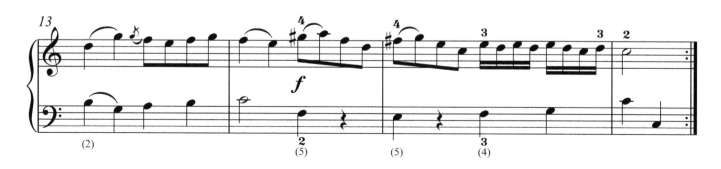

a) Grace note to be played on the beat.
Non-slurred quarter and eighth notes may be played detached.

List B

# German Dance in A

WoO 42

Ludwig van Beethoven
(1770–1827)

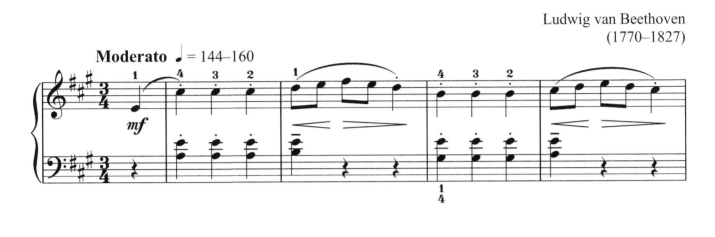

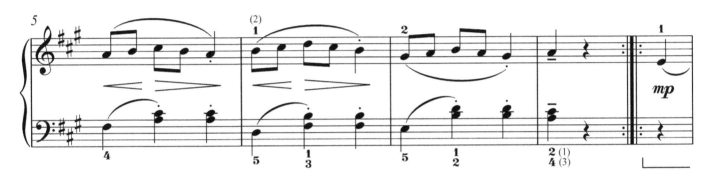

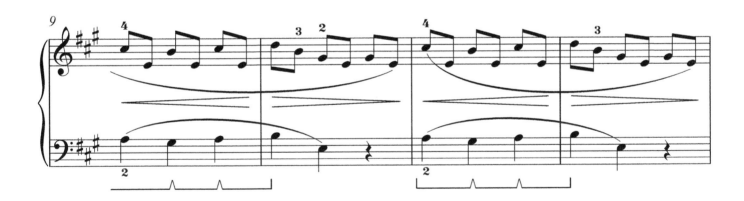

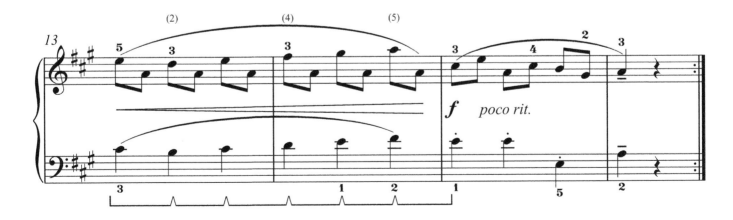

# Sonatina in G

Thomas Attwood
(1765–1838)

a) Grace note to be played on the beat.

# Ecossaise in G

## WoO 23

Ludwig van Beethoven
(1770–1827)

# Minuet in G

from *Sonata*, Hob. XVI:8

Franz Joseph Haydn
(1732–1809)

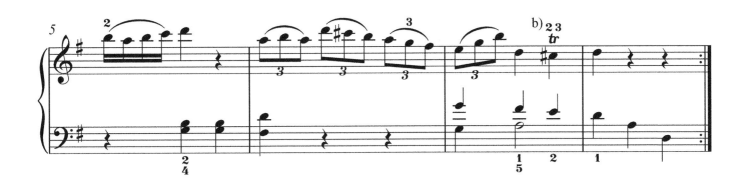

# Sonatina in C

## Op. 36, No. 1 (1st movement)

Muzio Clementi
(1752–1832)

**List B**

# Allegro in B Flat

K 3

Wolfgang Amadeus Mozart
(1756–1791)

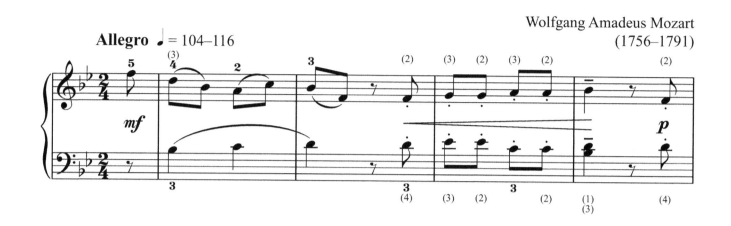

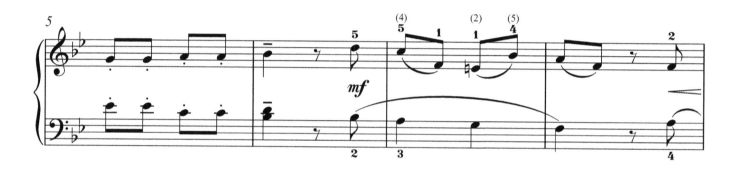

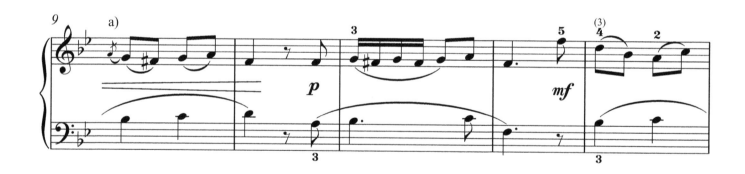

a) Grace note to be played on the beat.

# Country Dance in B Flat

Wolfgang Amadeus Mozart
(1756–1791)

**List B**

# Contemplation in F

Daniel Gottlob Türk
(1756–1813)

a) Grace notes to be played on the beat.

# Sonatina
### Op. 157, No. 4 (1st movement)

Fritz Spindler
(1817–1905)

**Allegro moderato** ♩ = 84–96

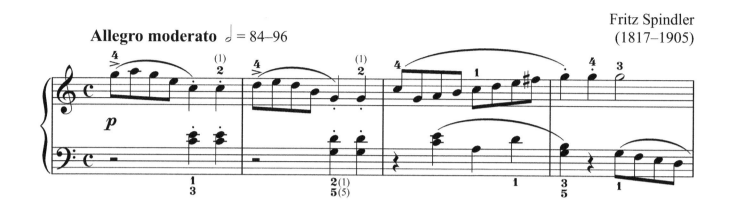

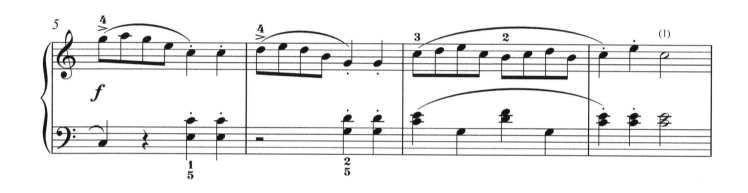

# Little Suite No. 4 in F

Johann Georg Witthauer
(1750–1802)

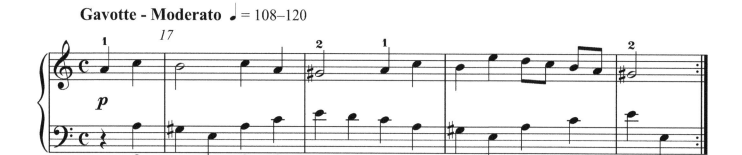

# NIGHT SKY

Christopher Norton
(1953-   )

List C

# Reverie

*Jean Ethridge
(1943–    )

# The Elegant Toreador

from *Moodscapes*

Seymour Bernstein
(1927– )

**Flirtatiously** ♩ = 58–69

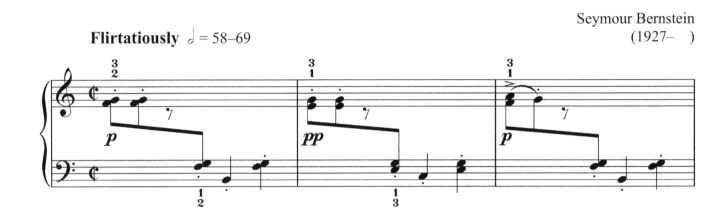

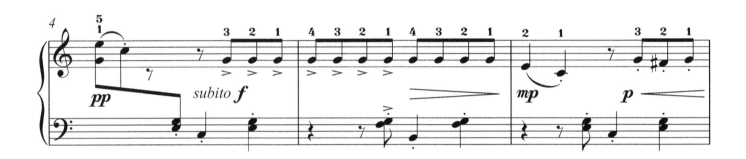

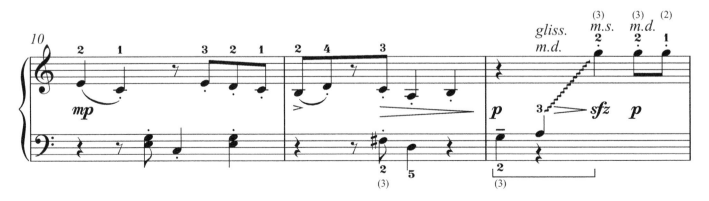

# The "Wrong Notes" Dance

*Rémi Bouchard
(1936–   )

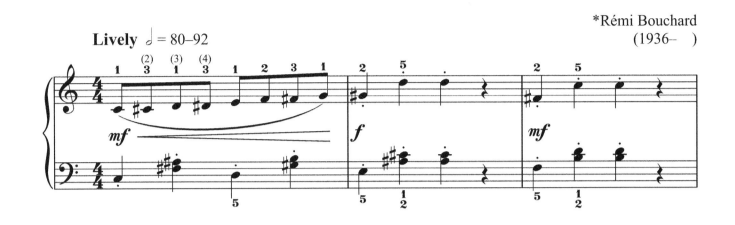

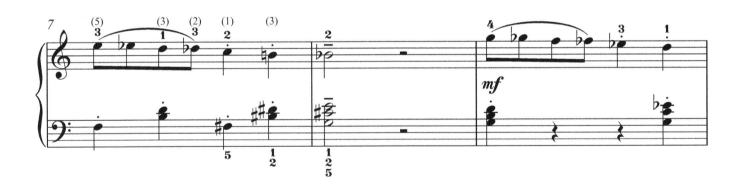

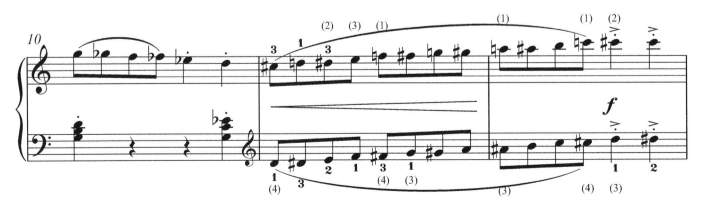

# Morning Walk

from *Glass Beads*, Op. 123, No. 1

Alexander Gretchaninov
(1864–1956)

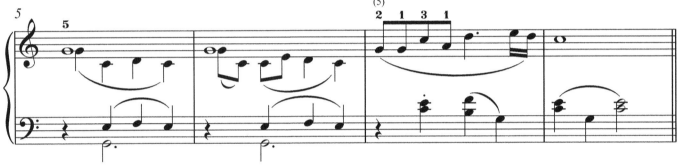

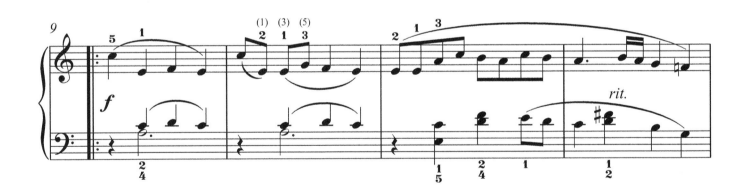

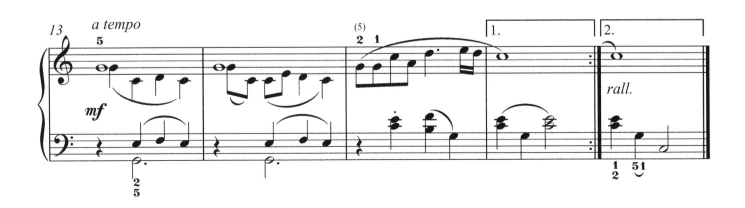

List C

# Clowns

Op. 39, No. 20

Dmitry Borisovich Kabalevsky
(1904–1987)

# Old MacDonald Had "Some" Farm

### (Five Variations on a Familiar Theme)

Mark Nevin
(1900–    )

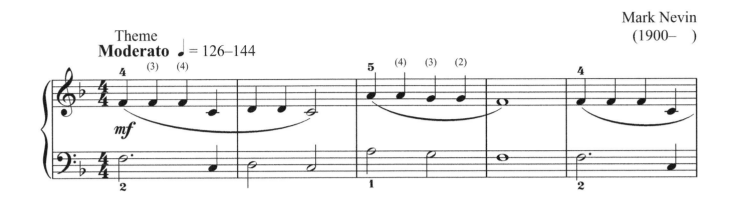

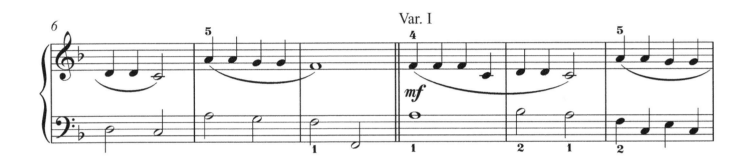

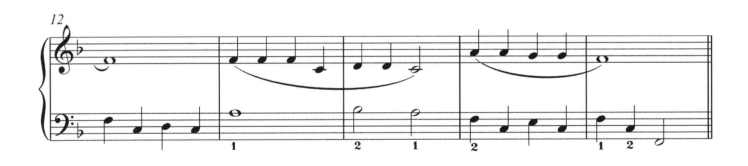

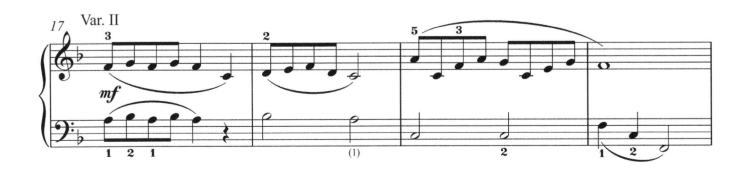

42

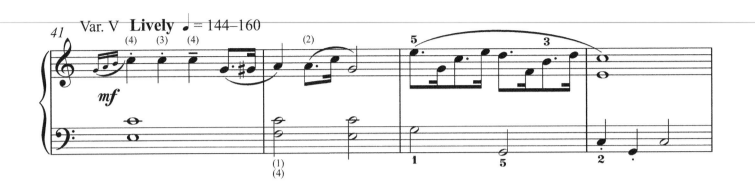

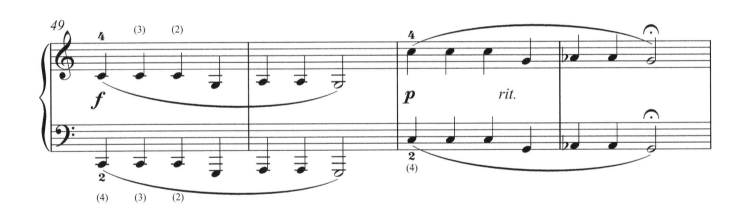

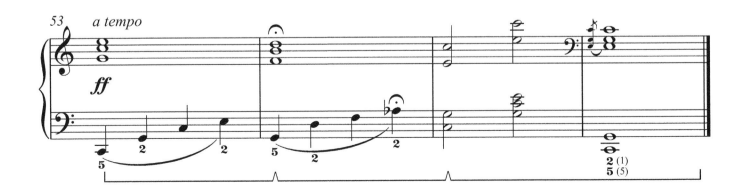

**List C**

# Picnic Piece
from *Microjazz I*

Christopher Norton
(1953–   )

# Rhumba

*Andrew Harbridge
(1966–   )

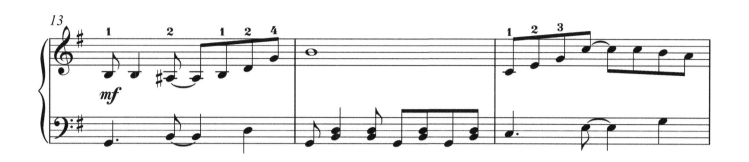

**List C**

# Spain

*Clifford Poole
(1916–2003)

# Blue Boogie

from *A Splash of Color, Book 1*

Denis Alexander
(1947–    )

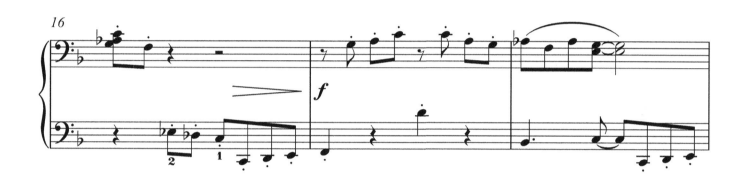

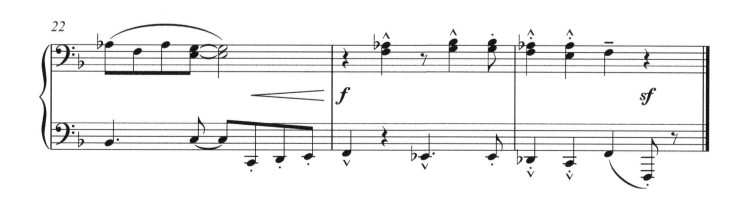

# Richard's Rag

*D.F. Cook
(1937–   )

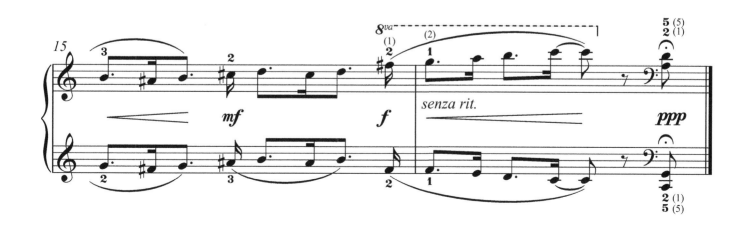

**Study**

# ANDANTE

Cornelius Gurlitt
(1820-1901)

**Study**

# Etude in A Minor

Carl Czerny
(1791–1857)

a) Grade note to be played on the beat.

# Hunting Song

James Hook
(1746–1827)

Study

# The Three Woodpeckers

Johann Nepomuk Hummel
(1778–1837)

# GATHERING PACE

Christopher Norton
(1953-    )

# Pagoda

Lynn Freeman Olson
(1938–1987)

**Study**

# Let's Make Up

William Scher
(1900–1975)

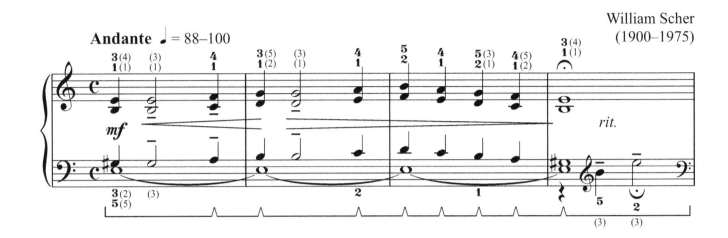

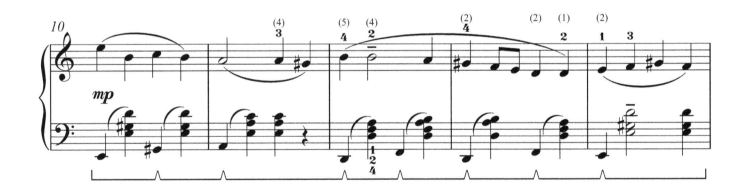

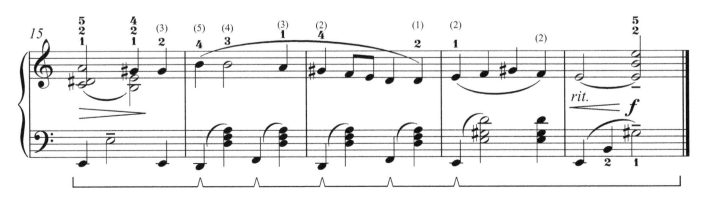

# Glossary of Composers

## About The Composers In Grade Three

Students are encouraged to explore online resources to expand their individual knowledge of the composers listed.

**ALCON, Susan** (born 1953). U.S.A. Alcon is a native of Greensboro, North Carolina where she teaches, composes and works as an adjudicator. Her compositions include jazz and pop styles with lyrical and Romantic methods.

**ALEXANDER, Dennis** (born 1947). U.S.A. Alexander is a performer, adjudicator, clinician and composer who currently teaches piano performance and pedagogy at the University of Montana. He composed the imaginative collection *A Splash of Color* with the junior/intermediate piano student in mind.

**ARNOLD, Samuel** (1740-1802). BRITAIN. Arnold was a composer, editor and organist at the Chapel Royal and Westminster Abbey. He was actively involved in theatrical entertainments and composed much music for the theatre. He also edited and published the works of Händel in 36 volumes.

**ATTWOOD, Thomas** (1765-1838). BRITAIN. Attwood was a composer and organist who wrote anthems for the coronations of George IV and William IV. He studied with Mozart in Vienna and was a friend of Mendelssohn. He also wrote preludes and fugues for the organ, as well as sonatinas for the young pianist.

**BACH, Johann Sebastian** (1685-1750). GERMANY. Bach was born into a family that had been musicians for nearly 200 years. Bach's first teacher was his father. He died when Bach was only ten, so Bach went to live and study with his older brother. Throughout his life, Bach worked as an organist, violinist, teacher and composer. He married twice and had 20 children, ten of whom died in infancy. Four of his sons became famous musicians. During his lifetime, Bach was famous as an organist, but we remember him today as a composer of music for church, orchestra, choir, organ and keyboard. His *Anna Magdalena's Notebook* was a gift he gave his second wife on her 24th birthday. It's filled with family favourites, ideal for the young pianist.

**BEETHOVEN, Ludwig van** (1770-1827). GERMANY. Beethoven had a great influence upon the development of music from the Classical style to the Romantic. His life was difficult, but even his deafness in later life did not stop him from composing. His nine symphonies changed orchestral music forever, and his piano works are considered among the most important repertoire ever composed for that instrument. Most of Beethoven's music is intended for experienced performers; however the *Russian Folk Song* in this book will give young pianists an introduction to his style.

**BERNSTEIN, Seymour** (born 1927). U.S.A. Bernstein is a composer, pianist, teacher, writer and lecturer in New York City. He has toured the world as a concert pianist. His children's piano music has appealing titles and is written in many styles from Romantic to avante-garde.

**\*BOUCHARD, Rémi** (born 1936). CANADA. Bouchard is a composer, adjudicator, workshop clinician and teacher. Born in Laurier, Manitoba, he studied at the University of Manitoba. His choral music has been performed in Canada and Finland, and his piano pieces are heard often throughout North America. He now lives and teaches in Neepawa, Manitoba.

**CLARKE, Jeremiah** (c1674-1707). BRITAIN. Clarke was a composer and organist who studied with John Blow at the Chapel Royal. Clarke held organist posts at Westminster Abbey, St. Paul's Cathedral and the Chapel Royal. He is most famous for his anthems and odes for choir, although he composed some keyboard music. Today, his famous *Trumpet Voluntary* is a popular piece at weddings.

**CLEMENTI, Muzio** (1752-1832). BRITAIN. Born in Rome, Italy, Clementi displayed such unusual musical talent that at the early age of 14 he was sent to England to continue his studies. He soon became the toast of London as a concert pianist and composer. Though he travelled extensively throughout Europe giving concerts, he made London his home where he earned a reputation as a successful composer, conductor, teacher, pianist, music publisher and piano manufacturer. Clementi was one of the first to compose pieces for the then new pianoforte, and composed 64 piano sonatas. He knew Haydn, Mozart and Beethoven. Beethoven was particularly fond of Clementi's sonatas and was influenced by them.

**\*COOK, Donald F.** (born 1937). CANADA. Cook grew up and received his early music training in St. John's, Newfoundland. After further studies in New York City and London, England, Dr. Cook returned to Newfoundland to become the founding director of the

School of Music at Memorial University. Since 1992, he has served as Principal of Western Ontario Conservatory (now, CONSERVATORY CANADA ™).

**COUPERIN, François** (1668-1733). FRANCE. The Couperin family had been musicians for five generations when François was born. He was an organist, harpsichordist and composer. Couperin's harpsichord music was quite original and often had descriptive titles suggesting Romantic ideas. He also wrote instrumental music, secular songs and church works.

**\*CROSBY, Anne** (born 1968). CANADA. Crosby lives in Wolfville, Nova Scotia where she teaches piano and composes music for young pianists. She studied piano performance and pedagogy at Acadia University in Wolfville, Nova Scotia, and at the University of Michigan. Crosby is also an examiner for Conservatory Canada.

**CZERNY, Carl** (1791-1857). AUSTRIA. Czerny was the son of a Czech piano teacher who settled in Vienna, Austria. He was taught by his father and Beethoven. Czerny was a dedicated piano teacher; one of his most famous pupils was Franz Liszt. Czerny composed over 1,000 works, many of which are technical piano pieces.

**DANDRIEU, Jean-Francois** (1682-1738). FRANCE. Dandrieu was a harpsichordist, composer and organist at the Royal Chapel in Paris. He wrote three collections of harpsichord music of a descriptive nature, containing short and charming pieces similar to those by Couperin. He also composed for organ and chamber ensemble.

**\*ETHRIDGE, Jean** (born 1943). CANADA. Ethridge was born in Rossland, British Columbia. She studied music at the University of British Columbia, and at the Royal College of Music in London, England. Her composition teachers included well-known Canadian composers Jean Coulthard, Murray Adaskin and Violet Archer. Ethridge's works include orchestral, piano, chamber and vocal music.

**GRETCHANINOV, Alexander Tikhonovich** (1864-1956). U.S.A. Born in Russia, Gretchaninov studied composition in Moscow with Rimsky-Korsakov. He toured Europe, lived in Paris and finally settled on New York City where he died in 1956. Tchaikovsky's influence can be heard in Gretchaninov's music, which includes string quartets, chamber music, incidental music, songs, and piano pieces (especially for children).

**HÄNDEL, Georg Friedrich** (1685-1759). GERMANY AND ENGLAND. Händel showed early musical talent, but his father was opposed to him becoming a musician. His father reluctantly allowed Händel to study organ, and soon afterward he became a violinist at an opera house. As a young man, Händel left his native Hanover, Germany to spend several years in Italy. He settled in London, England in 1711 and enjoyed a long and successful career there as a composer of Italian opera and English oratorios.

**HAYDN, Franz Joseph** (1732-1809). AUSTRIA. At the age of eight, Haydn was accepted as a chorister at St. Stephen's Cathedral in Vienna, where he received his early musical education. He spent most of his working life as music director and composer for Prince Esterhazy, during which time Haydn composed orchestra works, church music, chamber music, keyboard music and solo songs. He is considered to be the Father of the Symphony, and, because he lived to a ripe old age, was lovingly referred to as "Papa Haydn".

**HOOK, James** (1746-1827). BRITAIN. Hook was a composer and organist at the famous Vauxhall Gardens, a popular gathering and entertainment place for fashionable Londoners in the late 18th century. He wrote stage works, concertos, sonatas, choral works and more than 2,000 songs.

**HUMMEL, Johann Nepomuk** (1778-1837). AUSTRIA. A student of Mozart, Haydn and Clementi, Hummel was a child prodigy and became famous throughout Europe as a virtuoso pianist. He wrote concertos, operas, chamber music, choral music and keyboard pieces. His most popular piece today is his *Trumpet Concerto*.

**KABALEVSKY, Dmitry Borisovich** (1904-1987). RUSSIA. Kabalevsky studied and later taught at the Moscow Conservatory. He composed chamber music, orchestral and choral music, and operas. His piano music for children is delightfully rhythmic and often humourous.

**MOZART, Wolfgang Amadeus** (1756-1791). AUSTRIA. Mozart was a child prodigy, performing, composing and touring Europe at an early age. He worked as a composer and pianist, but died at a young age and in poverty. His musical genius is evident in his operas, symphonies, concertos, chamber music and piano sonatas.

**NEVIN, Mark** (born 1900). U.S.A. Nevin, also known as Maurice Albert Levin, was born in New Jersey and studied at Princeton and Julliard. He is a composer, clinican and teacher who wrote educational works. His *Mark Nevin Piano Course* and *Piano for Adults* are comprehensive method books.

**\*NIAMATH, Linda** (born 1939). CANADA. A native of Vancouver, British Columbia, Niamath began piano studies at the age of five and by then was already beginning to compose. She taught elementary school and now teaches in her private studio. Most of her piano music was written for her own students. These pieces are expressive and imaginative character pieces.

**NORTON, Christopher** (born 1953). NEW ZEALAND. Norton is a teacher, composer and pianist. He moved to England in 1977 and wrote musicals, ballet scores, orchestral music and piano pieces. He composed the piano series *Microjazz* to help students understand and enjoy blues, jazz and rock styles.

**OLSON, Lynn Freeman** (1938-1987). U.S.A. Lynn Olson grew up in Minneapolis and graduated from the University of Minnesota. He studied piano with Frances Clark and composition with David Kraehenbuehl. His entire life was devoted to the music education of young people, and he composed a number of children's songs and piano pieces.

**PACHELBEL, Johann** (1653-1706). GERMANY. Pachelbel was an organist, teacher and composer who was a friend of J.S. Bach's father. Pachelbel is probably most famous for his *Canon in D*, but he also composed harpsichord suites, chorale preludes, motets, arias, concertos and cantatas. Unfortunately, the scores for many of his pieces have been lost.

**\*PATERSON, Lorna** (born 1953). CANADA. Paterson is a composer, teacher, adjudicator and pianist from Brentwood Bay, British Columbia. She composes piano music for children, and teaches at the Victoria Conservatory of Music. She also serves as an examiner for Conservatory Canada.

**\*POOLE, Clifford** (1916-2003). CANADA. Born in England, Poole came to Canada with his family at the age of nine. He and wife, Margaret Parsons, toured North America as a piano duo from 1954 to 1965. He taught at Western Ontario Conservatory, serving as its principal (1957-60), and later taught at The Royal Conservatory of Music in Toronto. Poole had a distinguished career in Toronto as a pianist, teacher, conductor, editor and composer. Some of his nine piano pieces appear under the pseudonyms of Charles Peerson, Ernest Marsen and J. Bach.

**PURCELL, Henry** (1659-1695). BRITAIN. Purcell was perhaps the most gifted English composer of his time. He was trained as a chorister under John Blow at the Chapel Royal and later at Westminster Abbey, succeeding him as organist there. Purcell composed theatre music, church music, solo songs and instrumental music. He died at the early age of 36 and is buried in Westminster Abbey.

**SCHER, William** (1900-1975). U.S.A. Scher was born in New York and studied with Lazar, Weiner and Zemachen. He pursued a career in music education, but wrote popular piano works such as *C Fantasy for 2 Pianos* and *Czarda*.

**SPINDLER, Fritz** (1817-1905). GERMANY. Spindler, himself a pianist, composed chiefly salon music and character pieces. His works blended both the Classical and Romantic styles. His *Sonatinas, Op. 157* are his most popular works with students.

**TELEMANN, Georg Philipp** (1681-1767). GERMANY. A composer and organist, Telemann was more famous during his lifetime than J.S. Bach. He was very active organizing and promoting concerts in Leipzig and later in Hamburg. His compositions included cantatas, passions, oratorios, operas, chamber music, harpsichord and organ music.

**TÜRK, Daniel Gottlob** (1756-1813). GERMANY. Türk was a composer, violinist and teacher. He was one of the first to write instructional pieces for children. His 160 piano pieces from *Pieces for Aspiring Players* have been compared to Schumann's *Album for the Young*.

**WITTHAUER, Johann Georg** (1750-1802). GERMANY. Witthauer began his career as a keyboard teacher and church organist in the city of Hamburg. In 1791 he accepted the post of organist at a church in Lübeck where he lived until his death. Witthauer composed several sets of sonatas for keyboard.

# O Canada

*Written in French by Adophe-Basile Routhier (1839-1920) in Quebec City and first
performed there in 1880 to a musical setting by Calixa Lavallée. Translated into English in
1908 by Robert Stanley Weir (1858-1926). Approved as Canada's national anthem by the
Parliament of Canada in 1967 and officially adopted in 1980.*

*Calixa Lavallée
(1842–1891)
*arr. D.F. Cook

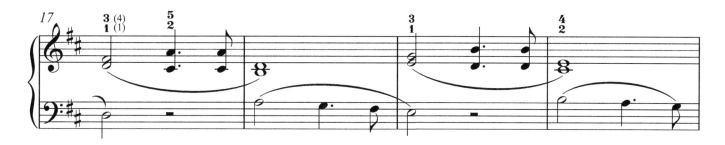

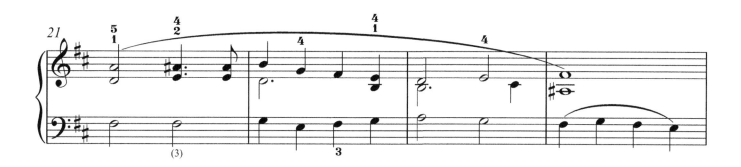

Ô Canada! Terre de nos aïeux,
Ton front est ceint de fleurons glorieux!

Car ton bras sait porter l'épée,
Il sait porter la croix!

Ton histoire est une épopée
Des plus brillants exploits.

Et ta valeur, de foi trempée,
Protégera nos foyers et nos droits.

Protégera nos foyers et nos droits.

O Canada! Our home and native land!
True patriot love in all of us command.

With glowing hearts we see thee rise,
The True North strong and free!

From far and wide,
O Canada, we stand on guard for thee.

God keep our land glorious and free!
O Canada, we stand on guard for thee.

O Canada, we stand on guard for thee.

CONSERVATORY CANADA™ conducts accredited music examinations in both Classical and Contemporary Idioms™ in many disciplines throughout Canada–from grades/levels 1 to 10 on through to professional Associate and Licentiate Diplomas.

For information about CONSERVATORY CANADA™ and our examination programs, please contact:

Office of the Registrar
Conservatory Canada
45 King Street, Suite 61
London, Ontario, Canada
N6A 1B8

Telephone: 519-433-3147
Toll free in Canada: 1-800-461-5367

Fax: 519-433-7404

Email: officeadmin@conservatorycanada.ca

www.conservatorycanada.ca